CHRISTMA COOKING
for Family and Friends

Sharing the festivities with family and friends is one of the greatest joys of Christmas, and whether this means a large-scale gathering of the clan, or a quiet celebration with the one you love, you'll find the key to a stress-free holiday within the pages of this book. Present needs are neatly met with a selection of edible gifts, and there are plenty of suggestions for setting the scene, including table decorations and festive napkin rings. On the food front, you'll find detailed instructions for cooking a traditional Christmas dinner, with alternative desserts to appeal to all members of the family. A special menu caters for couples who might prefer a sophisticated dinner à deux, and vegetarian guests are well provided for with a delicious mushroom and hazelnut roulade, a filo loaf with ribboned vegetable filling and a variety of egg and cheese-based treats. The feasting continues with a Boxing Day buffet and a midweek party which proves that leftovers can have an entirely new lease of life when given the right treatment. The week's entertaining is brought to an elegant close with a menu which provides a last opportunity for indulgence before the implementation of those New Year Resolutions!

CONTENTS

GIFTS AND DECORATIONS	3
FAMILY CHRISTMAS	8
TWO'S COMPANY	22
VEGETARIAN CHOICE	27
BOXING DAY	31
TEATIME TREATS	34
MIDWEEK CELEBRATION	38
NEW YEAR'S EVE PARTY	40
INDEX	48

Glazed Christmas Cake

GIFTS AND DECORATIONS

This chapter is packed with ideas for perfect presents, from incredible edibles to beautiful table decorations. Whether you make them for friends or save them for yourself, they are certain to prove popular.

Glazed Christmas Cake

The traditional iced cake, complete with snow scene, is not to everyone's taste. The glowing colours of this glazed rich fruit cake make it a gourmet gift.

250g (8oz) sultanas

250g (8oz) currants

250g (8oz) raisins

125g (4oz) chopped mixed candied peel

250g (8oz) glacé cherries

60g (2oz) glacé pineapple

60g (2oz) pitted dates

6 tblspn brandy

250g (8oz) butter or margarine, softened

155g (5oz) soft brown sugar

5 eggs

60g (2oz) dark chocolate

1 tspn vanilla essence

2 tspn glycerine

2 tspn raspberry jam

finely grated rind and juice of 1 lemon

250g (8oz) plain flour

1 tspn mixed spice

1 tspn ground ginger

¼ tspn salt

Topping

4 tblspn apricot jam

12 red glacé cherries

20-22 blanched almonds

8 green glacé cherries

22-24 pecan nuts

1 Line and grease a 20cm (8in) round or square cake tin. Combine the sultanas, currants, raisins and mixed peel in a bowl. Using kitchen scissors, cut the cherries, pineapple and dates into small pieces; add them to the bowl. Stir in 4 tablespoons of the brandy and mix well. Cover the bowl and leave overnight.

2 Preheat oven to 150°C (300°F/Gas 2). Beat the butter or margarine in a mixing bowl until light and creamy. Add the brown sugar and beat with a hand-held electric mixer until light and fluffy. Add the eggs one at a time, beating well after each addition, and adding a little of the flour if the mixture shows signs of curdling.

3 Melt the chocolate in a heatproof bowl over a saucepan of simmering water. Remove from the heat and cool slightly, then add to the cake mixture, with the vanilla essence, glycerine, raspberry jam and finely grated lemon rind and juice.

4 Sift the flour, mixed spice, ginger and salt into a bowl. Gradually add the dry ingredients to the creamed mixture, alternately with the soaked fruit, ending with flour. Mix well.

5 Spoon the mixture into the prepared cake tin and smooth the surface. Bang the tin lightly on a flat surface to break up any air bubbles. Bake for 3-3½ hours, or until the cake is firm to the touch. A skewer, inserted in the cake, should come out clean.

6 Remove the cake from the oven, prick the surface with a fine skewer and sprinkle with the remaining brandy. Cool in the tin on a wire rack, then remove the cake from the tin. Leaving the lining paper in place, overwrap in a double thickness of foil and store in an airtight container.

7 To decorate, remove the wrappings and stand the cake on a wire rack. Melt the apricot jam in a small saucepan. Press the jam through a sieve into a heatproof bowl. Brush half the apricot glaze over the surface of the cake. Arrange 4 glacé cherries in the centre of the cake, surrounding them with a stockade of blanched almonds. Add a circle of green and red glacé cherries and a necklace of almonds. Finally press pecan nuts into the glaze to form a decorative rim. Using a clean brush, lightly coat the decoration with the rest of the apricot glaze.
Serves 24-30

Kitchen Tip
When cutting up the cherries, glacé pineapple and dates, dip the scissors frequently into a jug of boiling water; this will prevent the fruit from sticking to the blades.

Fruit and Nut Caramels

185g (6oz) glacé cherries, chopped

90g (3oz) no-need-to-soak dried apricots

155g (5oz) whole mixed nuts

220g (7oz) caster sugar

90g (3oz) butter or margarine

2 tblspn golden syrup

4 tblspn liquid glucose

125ml (4fl oz) condensed milk

1 Grease a 28 x 18cm (11 x 7in) cake tin. Spread the cherries, apricots and mixed nuts evenly over the bottom of the tin.

2 Combine all the remaining ingredients in a heavy-based saucepan. Heat gently, stirring until the sugar has dissolved. Raise the heat to moderate and continue cooking the mixture, stirring constantly, for about 10 minutes, or until it turns a deep golden colour and starts to come away from the sides of the pan.

3 Pour the caramel mixture over the fruit and nuts. Leave for about 1 hour until set, then chop into small pieces, using a cleaver or heavy knife. Store in an airtight container.

4 Arrange the caramels in paper or foil cases in a box lined with coloured cellophane or crumpled tissue paper.

Makes about 70 pieces

Shortbread Jewels

250g (8oz) butter, softened

155g (5oz) caster sugar

60g (2oz) ground rice

375g (12oz) plain flour, sifted

60g (2oz) red glacé cherries

60g (2oz) green glacé cherries

125g (4oz) blanched almonds

1 Preheat oven to 180°C (350°F/ Gas 4). Lightly grease a 30 x 25cm (12 x 10in) Swiss roll tin.

2 Cream the butter with the sugar in a mixing bowl. Gradually work in the ground rice, then the plain flour, until the mixture forms a firm dough. Turn onto a floured surface and knead lightly for 2 minutes.

3 Press the dough evenly into the prepared tin and mark lightly into 5cm (2in) squares. Decorate each square with cherries and almonds. Bake for 30-40 minutes or until the shortbread jewels are cooked through and golden.

4 Cool the shortbread jewels in the tin on a wire rack before cutting into squares. Pack in an airtight tin, preferably one with a Christmas motif.

Makes 24

Peppermint Creams

1 large egg white

5 tblspn double cream

1-1½ teaspoons peppermint essence

625g (1¼ lb) icing sugar, sifted

green food colouring

icing sugar for dusting

1 Break up the egg white with a fork in a large mixing bowl. Using a wooden spoon, beat in the cream and 1 teaspoon of the peppermint essence.

2 Gradually stir in the icing sugar until the mixture is smooth and firm enough to handle. Add more peppermint essence, if liked, and work in enough of the green colouring to tint the mixture a pale green. Knead until the colouring is evenly distributed.

3 Dust a clean surface generously with icing sugar. Roll out the paste to a thickness of about 5mm (¼in). Cut out shapes – discs are traditional, but holly leaves would be more appropriate for a festive gift – and arrange on trays lined with nonstick baking paper. Leave to dry for 8-12 hours, turning once. Pack in a decorative box, separating the layers with sheets of tissue.

Makes about 625g (1¼lb)

Christmas Tree Biscuits

These brightly decorated biscuits make ideal presents to pack in boxes or hang on the tree.

375g (12oz) plain flour

2 tspn baking powder

2 tspn ground cinnamon

1 tspn mixed spice

1 tspn ground ginger

¼ tspn salt

250g (8oz) butter, softened

185g (6oz) soft brown sugar

3 tblspn brandy, rum or orange juice

1 egg white, lightly beaten

sultanas, raisins, almonds and glacé cherries to decorate

1 Preheat oven to 180°C (350°F/ Gas 4). Sift the flour, baking powder, cinnamon, mixed spice, ginger and salt into a bowl; set aside.

2 Cream the butter in a mixing bowl, using a wooden spoon or hand-held electric mixer. Gradually beat in the sugar, then add the brandy, rum or orange juice with a little of the flour. Stir in the remaining flour to make a soft dough. Wrap closely and chill for 30 minutes.

3 Roll out the dough on a lightly floured surface to a thickness of about 5mm (¼in). Using a tree-shaped biscuit cutter or a cardboard template, cut out about 45 biscuits, rerolling the dough as required.

4 Arrange the biscuits on lightly greased baking sheets. Brush with egg white and decorate with sultanas, raisins, almonds and cherries. Use the tip of an icing nozzle to make a hole in the top of each biscuit for the ribbon.

5 Bake for 15 minutes or until golden and firm to the touch. Cool on wire racks.

6 Thread silver and gold ribbons through the biscuits and tie neatly into bows for packing.

Makes about 45

Bishop's Bread

2 eggs
125g (4oz) caster sugar
125g (4oz) plain flour
1 tspn baking powder
¼ tspn salt
375g (12oz) mixed glacé fruit
125g (4oz) mixed red and green glacé cherries
375g (12oz) raisins
500g (1lb) shelled whole nuts
5 tblspn brandy, rum or orange liqueur

1 Preheat oven to 150°C (300°F/ Gas 2). Line and grease two 25 x 8 x 4cm (10 x 3 x 1½ in) loaf tins.

2 Beat the eggs with the sugar in a bowl. Sift the flour, baking powder and salt into a separate, larger bowl.

3 Using kitchen scissors dipped in hot water, cut the mixed glacé fruit to about the same size as the cherries. Add to the dry ingredients with the cherries and raisins and stir until well coated in the flour.

4 Add the egg mixture and mix well, then divide between the tins, pressing the mixture well into the corners. Bake for 1¼ hours or until firm to the touch.

5 Remove the loaves from the oven and drizzle both with brandy, rum or liqueur. Cool in the tins, then wrap in coloured foil and refrigerate until ready to present.
Makes 2 loaves

DECORATIONS

Sumptuous decorations set the scene for the festivities. Follow the step-by-step directions here and on page 22 for perfect results.

Wiring Cones, Nuts and Pine

Wiring items for table decorations and wreaths makes it easy to form natural-looking shapes and arrangements. The technique is simple:

Cones: Use 1.25mm (18 gauge) stub wires unless cones are very small, in which case 0.71mm (22 gauge) should be used. Loop the wire through the bottom row of bracts, bring the ends together and twist to form a stem.

Nuts: For walnuts, dip one end of 1.25mm (18 gauge) stub wire into an all-purpose glue; stick it onto the bottom of the nut. Wire harder nuts by looping the wire around them and twisting it to form a stem.

Pine: Strip off the bottom needles, then turn one end of a stub wire back and lay the flattened loop against the stem. Twist the longer end around the wire and stem.

Golden Advent Ring

green oasis ring and base
4 candle holders
1.25mm (18 gauge) stub wire
golden cherubs
pine fronds, about 10cm (4in) long
4 gold candles
wired grapes, cones, chestnuts, walnuts and brown ribbon bows

1 Soak the oasis ring by turning it upside down in a basin of water and leaving for 10 minutes.

2 Space the candle holders around the soaked oasis ring.

3 Wire the cherubs from the back, and arrange them around the oasis ring.

4 Strip the needles from the bottom 2.5cm (1in) of the pine stems. Push the pine tips into the ring at an angle of about 45° until the oasis is completely covered. Then add the candles (still in their plastic wrappings – these will help to protect the candles from any damage while the arrangement is being made).

5 Finally, arrange wired grapes, cones, nuts and bows to complete the ring. Remove the wrappings from the candles before lighting.

Studded Oranges

One of the most effective table decorations is also the simplest. All is takes is time, a bowl of oranges and a large supply of cloves. Stud the oranges with the cloves, covering them completely if you plan to keep the oranges for a long time – or creating a decorative effect by dividing each orange into eighths by means of cloves, so that the fruit resembles a panelled ball. Arrange the studded oranges in a simple glass bowl or on a glass cake stand. They will add fragrance as well as beauty to the festive table.

Pomanders

Studded oranges also make perfect pomanders. Ripe, thin-skinned oranges should be completely covered with cloves. Start at the stalk end and add the cloves in concentric circles until the entire fruit is evenly and neatly covered.

For each studded orange you will require 1 teaspoon each of ground cinnamon and orris powder. Roll the studded oranges in the mixture, making sure that they are completely coated. Wrap each pomander separately in paper towels and place in a dark cupboard for 10-14 days.

Press a tiny hook into the top of each orange and thread a narrow velvet ribbon through the hook so that the pomander may be hung from a door knob or coat hanger.

If made correctly, the pomander will not rot, but will merely shrivel as years go by.

Golden Advent Ring

Indoor Wreaths

Although the front door is the usual site for the holly wreath, these can also be used to great effect inside the house.

The basic ring, complete with green oasis, can be purchased from florists. Cover the ring with short sprays of evergreens, using one type only or a mixture. Any offcuts from the Christmas tree can be used, together with ivy, holly and cypress.

Keep the decoration natural, with cones and nuts, or add bows, baubles or tiny tree decorations in tones that complement your Christmas table colour scheme.

Alternatively, make a fabric wreath. Using Christmassy material, make three slim fabric tubes of equal width and length, stuffing each tube with terylene wadding. Arrange the tubes neatly side by side, sew them together at the top, then plait them tightly so that the plait forms a circle. Sew the joins together and add a bow to match one of the colours that predominates in the chosen fabric.

Apples and Nightlights

If this arrangement is too large for your dining table, it could be placed on a sideboard.

soaked green oasis

a large, low flat dish

wire netting

silver reel wire

pine fronds, about 15cm (6in) long

at least 20 bright red apples

10 nightlights

1.25mm (18 gauge) stub wires

1 Place the oasis in the dish, then trim off the corners with a sharp kitchen knife to make a mound. Cover the oasis mound with wire netting, securing it to the dish with silver reel wire.

2 Strip the lower needles from the pine fronds, then arrange them in the oasis at an angle of 45° until it is completely covered.

3 Polish the apples with a soft dry cloth until they are shiny.

4 With a sharp narrow-bladed knife, cut a hole large enough to accommodate a nightlight in the top of 10 of the apples. Carefully insert an unlit nightlight into each hole. Wire the apples by pushing a stub wire into the base and out the other side. Arrange all the apples in the oasis, securing in place with the stub wires.

5 Light the nightlights half an hour before the guests are due, but take care that no pine overhangs the candles, as this could prove a fire hazard.

Kissing Ring

The tradition of stealing a kiss under the mistletoe may stem from the Druid's belief that the plant was a symbol of fertility. In Victorian times, mistletoe was often bound on wire frames to form balls or kissing rings, which were suspended from the ceiling by red ribbons.

It was the custom that for every kiss exchanged under the mistletoe a berry must be removed.

FAMILY CHRISTMAS

It's a time for celebration – the gathering of the clan. However restrained the rest of the year may be, this is an occasion for indulgence. Our menu opens with a selection of starters, advances to perfect roast turkey, and concludes with flaming – or frozen – Christmas pudding and a variety of sweet treats.

Ham and Asparagus Gratins

24 large fresh asparagus spears, trimmed

12 slices of roast ham

60g (2oz) fresh white breadcrumbs

60g (2oz) flaked almonds

Sauce

90g (3oz) butter

90g (3oz) flour

900ml (1½pt) milk

185g (6oz) Gruyère or mature Cheddar cheese, grated

1 tblspn Dijon mustard

salt

freshly ground black pepper

1 Make the sauce. Melt the butter in a small saucepan. Stir in the flour and cook for 1 minute, then gradually add the milk, stirring until the sauce boils and thickens. Off the heat, stir in the cheese until melted. Add the mustard, with salt and pepper to taste; mix well.

2 Cook the asparagus in a tall pan of boiling water for 4 minutes, then drain.

3 Preheat oven to 190°C (375°F/ Gas 5). Cut the ham slices in half and wrap each piece around an asparagus spear. Arrange in a lightly greased baking dish, spoon over the sauce and top with the breadcrumbs and almonds.

4 Bake for 20 minutes or until the sauce is bubbling and the topping is crisp and golden. Serve.
Serves 8

Striped Salmon Terrine

375g (12oz) boneless salmon, skinned

1 egg white

155ml (5fl oz) double cream

lemon juice, see method

salt

freshly ground black pepper

375g (12oz) sole fillets, skinned

2 tblspn chopped fresh dill

1 tblspn chopped fresh tarragon or parsley

butter for greasing

salad leaves, herb sprigs and crème fraîche, to serve

1 Cut the salmon into 2.5cm (1in) pieces; purée in a blender or food processor until smooth. Add the egg white and blend again to mix. Transfer the mixture to a bowl, cover and chill for at least 30 minutes.

2 Return the salmon mixture to the blender or food processor and add the cream with lemon juice, salt and pepper to taste. Process until smooth. Return to the clean bowl, cover and chill for 30 minutes as before.

3 Cut the sole fillets into long strips and roll in the chopped herbs until coated.

4 Preheat oven to 180°C (350°F/ Gas 4). Grease a 600ml (1pt) loaf tin or terrine with butter. Spoon one third of the salmon mixture into the tin and spread evenly to fill the corners.

5 Lay the sole strips on top of the salmon, leaving a border all around. Carefully spoon over the remaining salmon mixture and level the surface.

6 Cover the tin with buttered foil and place in a roasting tin containing enough hot water to come halfway up the sides of the

terrine. Bake for 35 minutes, or until a fine skewer inserted in the centre of the terrine comes out clean.

7 Remove the terrine from the roasting tin. When cold, remove the foil, cover with oiled greaseproof paper and weight down with cans or a clean, well-wrapped house brick. Chill for at least 4 hours before turning out.

8 Slice the terrine and serve on individual plates, garnished with a variety of salad leaves and fresh herbs. Add a spoonful of crème fraîche to each plate.

Serves 6

Leek and Stilton Soufflé (page 27), Crispy Bacon and Avocado Salad (page 10), Ham and Asparagus Gratins, Striped Salmon Terrine

Crispy Bacon and Avocado Salad

Illustrated on page 9

2 avocados, sliced

12 rindless streaky bacon rashers, chopped

500g (1lb) mixed salad leaves

125g (4oz) hazelnuts, toasted and chopped

Dressing

6 tblspn hazelnut oil

2 tblspn cider vinegar

1 tspn Dijon mustard

2 cloves garlic, crushed

salt

freshly ground black pepper

1 Make the dressing by combining all the ingredients in a screw-top jar. Close the jar tightly and shake until well mixed.

2 Toss the avocado slices in the dressing in a bowl. Fry the bacon until crisp; add to the bowl with the salad leaves and hazelnuts. Toss and serve at once.
Serves 6-8

Perfect Roast Turkey

4.5kg (9lb) oven-ready turkey, thawed if frozen

30g (1oz) butter, melted

Rice and Nut Stuffing

315g (10oz) cooked brown rice

375g (12oz) minced pork or pork sausagemeat

½ bunch parsley, finely chopped

60g (2oz) flaked almonds, toasted

4 tblspn lemon juice

125g (4oz) sultanas

1 tspn dried mixed herbs

salt

freshly ground black pepper

Garnish

fresh rosemary sprigs

bay leaves

1 Preheat oven to 190°C (375°F/ Gas 5). Make the stuffing by combining all the ingredients in a large bowl; mix well until thoroughly combined.

2 Remove the giblets and neck from the turkey and use as the basis of Pan Gravy (page 12), if desired. Wipe the turkey inside and out with dampened paper towels, then dry.

3 Fill the neck cavity of the turkey loosely with one third of the stuffing. Shape the remaining stuffing into about 16 balls and place in an ovenproof dish. Chill until ready to cook. Truss the turkey, see page 12.

4 Place the turkey in a large roasting tin. Brush all over with the melted butter and season in salt and pepper. Roast for 2¼-2¾ hours until cooked. If any parts show signs of over-browning, cover with foil. (The bird may be cooked in foil if preferred, for timings see page 12).

5 Remove the turkey from the oven and allow to stand for 20 minutes. During this time, cook the stuffing balls in the oven until golden, covering them with foil if necessary.

6 Remove the trussing strings and skewer. Place the turkey on a warmed serving platter. Surround with the stuffing balls and add a rosemary and bay garnish. Serve.
Serves 8

Kitchen Tip
To check that the turkey is cooked, insert a metal skewer into the thickest part of each thigh in turn. The juices should run clear, with no trace of pink.

Perfect Roast Turkey, served with Rice and Nut Stuffing Balls, Bacon-wrapped Sausages (page 12), Pan Gravy (page 12), Bread Sauce (page 12), Spicy Cranberry Sauce (page 13) and seasonal vegetables

Pan Gravy

Illustrated on page 11

giblets and neck from turkey

1 bay leaf

5-6 black peppercorns

few onion slices

few parsley stalks

1.2 litres (2pt) water

30g (1oz) plain flour

salt

freshly ground black pepper

1 Combine the turkey giblets and neck, bay leaf, peppercorns, onion, parsley and measured water in a saucepan. Bring to the boil, then lower the heat and simmer for 1 hour. Strain the liquid; set it aside.

2 Having removed the turkey from the roasting tin, pour off the fat, leaving 4-5 tablespoons of the roasting juices. Place the tin over gentle heat, sprinkle the flour over and stir with a wooden spoon until smooth.

3 Gradually stir in the reserved liquid. Increase the heat to moderate and stir until the gravy boils and thickens. Add salt and pepper to taste, pour into a warmed gravyboat and serve.

Makes about 1 litre (1¾pt)

Quick Cumberland Sauce

4 tblspn redcurrant jelly

1 tblspn orange marmalade

6 tblspn freshly squeezed orange juice

2 tblspn lemon juice

4 tblspn port

1 Melt the redcurrant jelly in a small saucepan over low heat. Stir in the marmalade, citrus juices and port. Simmer for 1 minute, then allow to cool. Store in an airtight tub in the refrigerator.

Makes about 250ml (8fl oz)

Bread Sauce

Illustrated on page 11

6 whole cloves

1 onion, peeled

1 bay leaf

600ml (1pt) milk

90-125g (3-4oz) fresh white breadcrumbs

60g (2oz) butter, cubed

salt

freshly ground black pepper

grated nutmeg

2 tblspn single cream

1 Stick the cloves into the onion. Combine the onion, bay leaf and milk in a saucepan and bring to the boil. Remove from the heat, cover; set aside for 30 minutes.

2 Stir the breadcrumbs and butter into the pan. Cook the sauce over very gentle heat for 15-20 minutes. Remove onion and bay leaf; add salt, pepper and nutmeg to taste. Stir in the cream just before serving.

Makes about 500ml (16fl oz)

Bacon-wrapped Sausages

Illustrated on page 11

8 rindless streaky bacon rashers

16 small chipolata sausages

1 Preheat oven to 190°C (375°F/Gas 5). Place each bacon rasher in turn on a board and stretch it with the back of a knife. Cut each rasher in half.

2 Roll a half-rasher of bacon around each sausage. Place join-side down in a roasting tin and cook for 25-30 minutes.

Makes 16

TURKEY TIPS AND TIMES

To truss a turkey, place it breast-side down, pull the neck skin over the cavity and tuck the wingtips under. Secure the neck skin with a metal skewer, pinning the wings to the body at the same time. Turn the bird breast-up and pass a trussing needle threaded with fine string through the upper part of one drumstick, then through the body and through the other drumstick. Draw the thread through so that string protrudes from both drumsticks. Turn the bird over again; cross the string over the back. Cross the ends of the string and tie the drumsticks and 'parson's nose' together.

Roasting Chart

Times are based on an oven temperature of 190°C (375°F/Gas 5). Add an extra 15 minutes if the turkey is wrapped in foil.

OVEN-READY WEIGHT	TIMING
1.5-2.5kg (3-5lb)	1½-1¾ hours
3-3.5kg (6-7lb)	1¾-2 hours
4-4.5kg (8-9lb)	2-2½ hours
5-5.5kg (10-11lb)	2¼-2¾ hours
6-6.5kg (12-13lb)	2¾-3 hours
7-8.5kg (14-17lb)	3¼-3½ hours
9-11kg (18-22lb)	3½-3¾ hours
13kg (23lb plus)	3¾ hours plus

Apple and Hazelnut Stuffing

60g (2oz) butter

1 onion, chopped

1kg (2lb) cooking apples, peeled, cored and grated

finely grated rind and juice of 2 oranges

250g (8oz) fresh wholemeal breadcrumbs

1 tblspn chopped fresh thyme

90g (3oz) hazelnuts, chopped

salt

freshly ground black pepper

2 eggs, beaten

1 Melt the butter in a saucepan. Add the onion, apples, orange rind and juice. Cook over moderate heat until the onion and apples are tender. Set aside.

2 Mix the breadcrumbs, thyme and hazelnuts in a bowl. Add plenty of salt and pepper to taste. Tip the apple mixture into the bowl. Mix well, adding enough of the beaten egg to bind the mixture. Use as alternative stuffing in the recipe for Perfect Roast Turkey on page 10.

Sufficient to stuff neck cavity of a 4.5kg (9lb) turkey, and make 16 stuffing balls

Spicy Cranberry Sauce

Illustrated on page 11

315g (10oz) bottled or canned cranberry sauce

1 tspn grated fresh root ginger

1 tspn ground cardamom

½ tspn ground cinnamon

2 tspn Worcestershire sauce

1 Combine all the ingredients in a small saucepan. Stir until the mixture boils, then lower the heat and simmer for 1 minute. Cool, then store in an airtight container in the refrigerator until required.

Makes about 250ml (8fl oz)

Clockwise from top right: *Honey Apple Sauce, Spicy Cranberry Sauce, Quick Cumberland Sauce and Cherry Chutney*

Honey Apple Sauce

2 Bramley apples, peeled, cored and diced

2 tblspn water

2 tblspn honey

15g (½oz) butter

1 tspn grated lemon rind

pinch of ground cloves

1 Place the apples and measured water in a small saucepan. Bring to the boil, then cover the pan with a tight-fitting lid, lower the heat and simmer for 5 minutes or until the apples are very soft and pulpy.

2 Remove the pan from the heat and beat in the remaining ingredients. Cool, then store in an airtight container in the refrigerator.

Makes about 375ml (12fl oz)

Cherry Chutney

2 x 425g (14oz) cans pitted dark cherries

250ml (8fl oz) white wine vinegar

1 large onion, finely chopped

185g (6oz) granulated sugar

125g (4oz) sultanas

1 tblspn white mustard seeds

1 tblspn ground cinnamon

1 tblspn whole cloves

2 tspn salt

1 Drain the cherries, pouring the juice from one of the cans into a medium saucepan. Add all the cherries, with the vinegar, onion, sugar, sultanas, spices and salt. Mix well.

2 Bring to the boil, then cover the pan, lower the heat and simmer the chutney for about 1 hour, stirring occasionally. Remove the lid and cook for a further 45 minutes, or until thickened. Remove from the heat and cool. Store in an airtight container in the refrigerator.

Makes about 600ml (1pt)

Rosemary Potatoes

1kg (2lb) small potatoes (not new potatoes)

6 rosemary sprigs

3 tblspn olive oil

coarse sea salt

freshly ground black pepper

1 Preheat oven to 200°C (400°F/ Gas 6). Peel the potatoes and make deep parallel cuts in each, cutting almost but not quite through. Strip the rosemary leaves from 4 of the stalks; chop them finely.

2 Place the potatoes in a roasting tin. Sprinkle with the rosemary leaves and oil and add plenty of salt and pepper. Turn the potatoes to coat them thoroughly.

3 Roast for 1-1¼ hours or until golden brown and cooked through. Garnish with the remaining rosemary sprigs.
Serves 6

Kitchen Tip
An easy way to cut the potatoes is to place them next to a thin board. Cut down until the knife's progress is halted by the board; the cuts will be of equal depth.

Citrus Broccoli and Cauliflower

375g (12oz) cauliflower florets

375g (12oz) broccoli florets

Orange Sauce

185ml (6fl oz) fresh orange juice

3 tblspn tarragon vinegar

salt

freshly ground black pepper

375g (12oz) butter, cubed

about 125ml (4fl oz) hot vegetable stock

orange rind shreds to garnish

1 Steam or microwave the cauliflower and broccoli until crisp-tender. Drain and keep warm in a serving dish.

2 Make the sauce by combining the orange juice and vinegar in a small pan. Add salt and pepper to taste. Boil rapidly until reduced to about 2 tablespoons.

3 Remove the pan from the heat and whisk in the butter, a piece at a time, until smooth and creamy. If the sauce becomes too thick, whisk very briefly over the heat until creamy.

4 Gradually whisk in enough of the stock to yield a pouring consistency. Pour the sauce over the vegetables, garnish with orange rind shreds and serve.
Serves 6

Almond Brussels Sprouts

750g (1½lb) small Brussels sprouts

45g (1½oz) butter

45g (1½oz) flaked almonds

1 clove garlic, crushed

2 tspn finely grated lemon rind

2 tspn lemon juice

salt

freshly ground black pepper

1 Trim the Brussels sprouts and cut a small cross in the base of each. Cook in a saucepan of salted water until crisp-tender.

2 Meanwhile, melt the butter in a small frying pan; sauté the almonds and garlic until golden. Stir in the lemon rind and juice, with salt and pepper to taste.

3 Drain the Brussels sprouts, tip them into a serving dish and pour the almond mixture over the top. Mix lightly and serve.
Serves 6

Rosemary Potatoes, Almond Brussels Sprouts, Carrots and Celery (page 16) and Citrus Broccoli and Cauliflower

Carrots and Celery

Illustrated on page 15

750g (1½lb) carrots

6 celery sticks

1 onion

1 small red pepper, cored and seeded

1 tblspn olive oil

salt

freshly ground black pepper

finely sliced spring onions to garnish

1 Cut the carrots and celery into even-sized sticks. Dice the onion and pepper.

2 Heat the oil in a saucepan, add the onion and sauté for 4-5 minutes until softened.

3 Add the carrots and celery to the pan and stir well. Cover the pan and cook the vegetables gently for about 10 minutes, until crisp-tender.

4 Stir in the red pepper, with salt and pepper to taste. Sprinkle with the spring onions and serve.
Serves 6

Beans with Tomato

750g (1½lb) French beans, topped and tailed

4 tblspn olive oil

3 ripe tomatoes, skinned and chopped

salt

freshly ground black pepper

1 Bring a saucepan of salted water to the boil, add the French beans and cook until crisp-tender. Drain well.

2 Heat the oil in a frying pan, add the tomatoes and cook gently for about 5 minutes. Add the beans, with salt and pepper to taste. Cover and cook for 2-3 minutes.
Serves 6

Apricot Sherry Trifle

Trifle is always popular. Omit the jelly, if preferred. Make individual trifles for younger members of the family, substituting apricot nectar for the alcohol and layering the ingredients as for a sundae.

2 jam-filled Swiss rolls

125ml (4fl oz) sweet sherry, Marsala or port

2 x 411g (14½oz) cans apricot halves, drained

600ml (1pt) prepared custard

1 x 142g (4oz) packet raspberry or strawberry jelly, made up according to instructions and set in a shallow tin

300ml (10fl oz) double cream

1-2 tblspn icing sugar

To Decorate

fresh fruit

chopped nuts

1 Cut the Swiss rolls into 1cm (½in) slices and use half to line the base and sides of a glass bowl. Sprinkle the slices with half the sherry, Marsala or port.

2 Arrange half the apricots on top of the sponge and cover with half the custard.

3 Chop the jelly into cubes and sprinkle half over the custard, then add the remaining sponge slices in a single layer. Moisten with the remaining sherry, Marsala or port.

4 Add another layer of apricots. Pour the remaining custard over the top and smooth the surface, then add the remaining jelly cubes.

5 Beat the cream with the icing sugar in a separate bowl until thick. Spoon into a piping bag. Decorate the top of the trifle in a lattice pattern or with rosettes. Add fruit and nuts. Chill until ready to serve.
Serves 6-8

Iced Christmas Pudding

60g (2oz) sultanas

60g (2oz) currants

60g (2oz) raisins

125g (4oz) glacé cherries, chopped

60g (2oz) chopped mixed candied peel

30g (1oz) glacé pineapple or stem ginger, chopped

60ml (2fl oz) brandy

1 litre (13/4pt) vanilla ice cream

150ml (5fl oz) double cream

125g (4oz) flaked almonds, toasted

60g (2oz) chocolate chips

sifted cocoa, chocolate holly leaves (see Kitchen Tip) and red marzipan berries to decorate

1 Mix the dried fruits and brandy in a bowl, cover closely and set aside for several hours.

2 Soften the ice cream. Place in a large bowl and stir in the cream, almonds, chocolate chips and soaked fruit.

3 Spoon into a 1.8 litre (3pt) pudding basin, cover with freezer wrap and freeze overnight or until solid.

4 Remove the wrap and immerse the basin in hot – not boiling – water for 30 seconds. Unmould onto a chilled serving plate. Dust lightly with sifted cocoa, add the chocolate holly leaves and marzipan berries and set aside to soften slightly before serving.
Serves 10-12

Kitchen Tip

To make the chocolate leaves, wash and dry several holly leaves (young leaves are easier to use). Brush the backs of the leaves with melted chocolate, then place, chocolate side up, on a baking sheet lined with nonstick baking paper. Refrigerate until set, then peel the leaves off the chocolate.

Iced Christmas Pudding

Traditional Christmas Pudding

185g (6oz) plain flour

1 tblspn mixed spice

185g (6oz) shredded suet

125g (4oz) soft brown sugar

125g (4oz) soft white breadcrumbs

grated rind and juice of 1 orange

1 cooking apple

90g (3oz) glacé cherries, roughly chopped

60g (2oz) flaked almonds

60g (2oz) hazelnuts

440g (14oz) currants

440g (14oz) raisins

375g (12oz) sultanas

60g (2oz) pitted dates, chopped

4 eggs, lightly beaten

250ml (8fl oz) brown ale

Orange and Brandy Butter or
Clear Brandy Sauce (recipes follow), to serve

1 Base line and grease two 1kg (2lb) pudding basins. Sift the flour and mixed spice together into a large bowl. Add the suet, sugar, breadcrumbs, orange rind and juice.

2 Peel and core the cooking apple. Grate it into the bowl. Stir in the cherries, nuts and fruits.

3 Add the eggs and brown ale and invite each member of the family to give the mixture a stir, making the traditional Christmas wish as they do so. Divide the mixture between the prepared basins and level the surfaces. Cover with circles of greaseproof paper, securing these under the rims with string. Cover with foil and tie again with string.

4 Place the puddings on upturned saucers in two large saucepans. Add boiling water to the pans to a depth of 7.5cm (3in). Cover with lids. Steam the puddings for 6 hours, topping up with boiling water as necessary. Cool, cover the puddings with fresh paper and foil and store in a cool place.

5 Reheat as described in Step 4 for 3-4 hours. Serve with Orange and Brandy Butter or Clear Brandy Sauce.
Each pudding serves 6-8

Orange and Brandy Butter

125g (4oz) butter, at room temperature

155g (5oz) icing sugar, sifted

2 tspn grated orange rind

1 tblspn brandy

1 Cream the butter in a bowl until very light and fluffy.

2 Gradually beat in the icing sugar until the mixture is very pale. Beat in the orange rind, then gradually add the brandy. Cover and refrigerate until required.
Serves 6-8

Clear Brandy Sauce

90g (3oz) soft brown sugar

2 tblspn cornflour

pinch salt

500 ml (16fl oz) water

2.5cm (1in) cinnamon stick

6 whole cloves

30g (1oz) butter

60ml (2fl oz) brandy

1 Combine the brown sugar, cornflour and salt in a medium saucepan off the heat. Gradually stir in the measured water.

2 Place over moderate heat and add the cinnamon stick and cloves. Bring to the boil, stirring, then lower the heat and simmer for 3 minutes. Remove the cinnamon and cloves. Stir in the butter, with enough of the brandy to give the desired flavour. Serve hot.
Serves 6-8

*Traditional Christmas Pudding
with Orange and Brandy Butter*

Mince Pies

The full flavour of the mincemeat develops on keeping, so try to make it at least a week before baking the mince pies.

125g (4oz) currants

125g (4oz) sultanas

125g (4oz) chopped mixed candied peel

125g (4oz) shredded suet

90g (3oz) blanched almonds, chopped

1 large Bramley apple, peeled, cored and grated

grated rind and juice of 2 lemons

grated rind and juice of 1 orange

1 x 227g (8oz) can crushed pineapple, drained

60g (2oz) soft brown sugar

1 tspn mixed spice

60ml (2fl oz) brandy

Pastry

125g (4oz) butter

125g (4oz) caster sugar

1 egg

125g (4oz) self-raising flour

125g (4oz) plain flour

1 egg white, lightly beaten

1 Combine all the ingredients for the mincemeat in a large bowl. Stir until well mixed. Spoon into clean jars, cover with tight-fitting lids and refrigerate until required.

2 Make the pastry. Cream the butter with the sugar in a mixing bowl. Beat in the egg, then sift the flours over the mixture and fold in. Knead the pastry lightly, wrap in clingfilm and chill for 1 hour.

3 Preheat oven to 180°C (350°F/ Gas 4). Roll the pastry out on a lightly floured surface and cut out twelve 7.5cm (3in) rounds with a fluted pastry cutter.

4 Fit the rounds into well-greased or nonstick tartlet cases or tins. Spoon a little of the mincemeat into each case, taking care not to over-fill them. Reroll the remaining pastry and cut lids. These may be plain, latticed or patterned, with the centres cut out using a star or Christmas tree cutter. If the lids are plain, make a small hole in the centre of each to allow the steam to escape.

5 Brush the pastry with egg white and bake the pies for 25 minutes or until golden. Cool for 2-3 minutes before transferring to wire racks to cool completely.
Makes 12

Filo Crackers

Filo Pastry comes in thin, ready-rolled sheets and is marvellously versatile. It is easy to use, but swiftly dries out when exposed to the air, so work swiftly and keep any unused sheets covered with clingfilm or a clean tea-towel.

12 sheets of filo pastry

60g (2oz) clarifed butter (see Kitchen Tips opposite), melted

Filling

60g (2oz) no-need-to-soak dried apricots

60g (2oz) glacé pineapple

60g (2oz) chopped dates

30g (1oz) red glacé cherries, chopped

30g (1oz) green glacé cherries, chopped

60g (2oz) flaked almonds

60g (2oz) ground almonds

¼ tspn ground cinnamon

1 tblspn finely grated lemon rind

1 tblspn caster sugar

1 tblspn melted butter

1 Preheat oven to 200°C (400°F/ Gas 6). Make the filling by mixing all the ingredients in a bowl so that the colours and flavours are well distributed.

2 Working with one sheet of filo at a time and keeping the rest covered, brush the surface lightly with melted clarified butter. Turn the filo, if necessary, so that a long edge faces you.

Chocolate Truffles, Mince Pies

3 Keeping the edge of the filo clear, spoon a thin 'sausage' of filling along the filo with within 7.5cm (3in) of either end.

4 Roll up the filo to make the cracker shape, twisting the unfilled ends. Snip them into tassels with sharp kitchen scissors, if liked.

5 Arrange the crackers on lightly greased baking sheets, brush them lightly with melted clarified butter and bake for 10-15 minutes or until golden. Serve warm.
Makes 12

Chocolate Truffles

You will require 25 small paper or foil cases for the truffles. Serve them on a china comport or flat cake stand, or pack them in boxes as gifts.

250g (8oz) dark chocolate, broken into pieces

4 tspn instant coffee powder

3 tblspn hot water

125g (4oz) butter, diced, at room temperature

3 tblspn coffee or chocolate-flavoured liqueur

about 60g (2oz) cocoa

1 Combine the chocolate, coffee powder and hot water in a heatproof bowl. Place over a saucepan of simmering water until the chocolate melts. Stir, then remove the bowl from the heat.

2 Using a wire whisk, beat the butter into the chocolate mixture, a piece at a time. When all the butter is incorporated, beat in the liqueur. Cover the bowl and chill the mixture until firm.

3 Sift the cocoa onto a sheet of greaseproof paper. Using a teaspoon, spoon out walnut-sized pieces of the chocolate mixture and shape them into balls.

4 Roll the balls in cocoa, then transfer them to the paper or foil cases. Chill until required.

Makes about 25

Kitchen Tips

Miniature bottles of liqueur are ideal for making these truffles. Brandy, whisky or sherry may be used instead of liqueur, if preferred.

Vary the appearance and flavour of the truffles by rolling them in finely grated white or dark chocolate, toasted coconut or finely chopped mixed nuts.

Clarify the butter for the filo crackers by melting it in a small saucepan, then setting it aside until the sediment falls to the bottom of the pan to leave a clear liquid on top. Carefully pour off this clear liquid – the clarified butter – discarding the solids in the pan.

TWO'S COMPANY

When you are cooking for two, or even for one, Christmas can be a sumptuous special event. With individual starters and sweets prepared in advance, this sophisticated menu allows plenty of time for setting a festive table, enjoying a glass or two of celebratory champagne and relishing a relaxing start to the day.

Holly and Nut Table Decoration

Napkin Garlands

Holly and Nut Table Decoration

This beautiful centrepiece adds a note of sophistication to the festive table.

soaked green oasis

1 black oasis tray

2 candle holders

green oasis tape

2 red candles

pine fronds and small holly branches

wired pine cones and nuts, see page 6

1 Place the oasis on the tray. trimming it to fit if necessary. Insert the candle holders into the top of the oasis, then tape the block to the tray, parcel-fashion.

2 Keeping the candles wrapped (for protection), place them on the holders.

3 Remove the tips from the pine fronds and strip the needles from the lower section of each. Insert the fronds into the oasis block until it is completely concealed.

4 Strip the lower leaves from the holly; insert the branches in the oasis. Add the wired cones, then complete the decoration with the nuts. Remove the wrappings from the candles before lighting and take care to keep them well away from the greenery.

Napkin Garlands

Sophisticated, simple or flamboyantly festive, napkin garlands may be made in a wide range of materials. Wire each item individually (see page 6) and cover bare stems with green floristry tape. If making these for a family party add the name of the recipient.

napkins

1.25mm (18 gauge) stub wire

green floristry tape

wired silver-sprayed pine cones, nuts and pine tips

1 Roll up a napkin; measure the circumference of the roll. Cut a length of stub wire to three quarters of the measured length, cover with green floristry tape and shape to fit the rolled napkin.

2 Carefully slide the wire off the napkin, then wire in pine cones, nuts and pine, or decorations of your choice. Fit the napkin garland onto the napkin.

Smoked Salmon Parcels

These individual starters look extremely elegant.

1 hard-boiled egg, finely chopped

60g (2oz) cream cheese

2 tblspn double cream

1 tspn snipped chives

salt

freshly ground black pepper

2 slices of smoked salmon

Dressing

2 tblspn olive oil

1 tblspn lemon juice

¼ tspn Dijon mustard

pinch of sugar

To Serve

2 whole chives

60g (2oz) mixed salad leaves

Melba Toast (page 40)

Smoked Salmon Parcels

1 Combine the chopped hard-boiled egg, cream cheese, cream and chives in a bowl. Mix well. Add salt and pepper to taste.

2 Lay the smoked salmon slices on a clean surface. Trim them, if necessary, to a neat rectangle. Divide the filling between them and roll up to make a neat parcel. Tie each parcel with a whole chive and arrange on individual plates. Cover with clingfilm and refrigerate until required.

3 Make the dressing. Combine all the ingredients in a small screwtop jar, close the lid tightly and shake well. Add salt and pepper to taste.

4 Just before serving, toss the salad leaves with the dressing in a bowl. Arrange the leaves on the plates with the salmon parcels. Serve with the Melba Toast.

Serves 2

French Roast Chicken with Cream Gravy

A layer of herb-flavoured cream cheese under the skin of this chicken keeps the flesh beautifully succulent and ensures that the carved breast meat looks as good as it tastes.

1 x 1.5kg (3lb) chicken

90g (3oz) cream cheese

2 tblspn chopped parsley

2 tspn chopped fresh or freeze-dried tarragon

1 small onion, finely chopped

30g (1oz) butter, softened

salt

freshly ground black pepper

250ml (8fl oz) white wine

250-300ml (8-10fl oz) chicken stock

1 tblspn cornflour

155ml (5fl oz) single cream

pinch of paprika

fresh herbs and celery leaves to garnish

Stuffing

30g (1oz) butter

1 small onion, finely chopped

2 sticks celery, finely chopped

2 tspn chopped fresh or freeze-dried tarragon

2 tblspn chopped fresh parsley

1 tspn grated lemon rind

125g (4oz) fresh white breadcrumbs

1 Preheat oven to 180°C (350°F/ Gas 4). Remove any excess fat from inside the chicken.

2 Place the cheese in a bowl. Add the parsley, tarragon and onion, with half the butter. Mix well, adding salt and pepper to taste.

3 Very gently ease the chicken skin away from the meat on the breast to create a pocket. Fill with the herby cheese mixture, then press down gently on the chicken skin to distribute the filling evenly.

4 Make the stuffing. Melt the butter in a small saucepan. Add the onion and fry gently until softened. Spoon into a bowl, add the remaining stuffing ingredients and mix well. Spoon into the neck cavity and close the cavity with trussing pins.

5 Truss the chicken, following the directions given for turkey on page 12. Place, breast-side up, on a wire rack over a roasting tin. Add the wine, 250ml (8fl oz) of the stock and the remaining butter to the tin. Roast the chicken for 1¼-1½ hours until golden and cooked. Baste the bird frequently during cooking, and turn the bird two or three times, finally roasting breast-side up for the last 15 minutes. Test by piercing the thickest part of one of the thighs with a skewer; the juices should run clear.

6 Transfer the chicken to a heated platter and rest for 5 minutes before carving. Meanwhile make the gravy. Skim off the fat from the liquid in the roasting tin; bring the remaining liquid to the boil, stirring to incorporate any sediment on the base of the tin and adding the extra stock, if necessary, to make a total of about 375ml (12fl oz).

7 In a jug, mix the cornflour with the cream until smooth. Stir in about 60ml (2fl oz) of the hot liquid, then add the contents of the jug to the roasting tin. Stir the mixture over the heat until the gravy is smooth and thickened. Add salt and pepper to taste.

8 Remove the trussing pins and strings from the chicken; add the garnish. Carve onto heated plates, spoon a little gravy over each portion and pour the remaining gravy into a sauceboat. Sprinkle the surface with the paprika and serve with the chicken and vegetables. Any leftover chicken will be delicious cold.
Serves 4

Kitchen Tip

The easiest way to chop the parsley for the stuffing is to place it in a mug and snip it with a pair of sharp kitchen scissors.

Railroad Potatoes

2 small baking potatoes

vegetable oil

salt

1 Preheat oven to 180°C (350°F/ Gas 4). Peel the potatoes and parboil them in a saucepan of boiling water for 5 minutes. Drain well and score the surface all over with the tines of a fork.

2 Pour vegetable oil into a small roasting tin to a depth of about 1cm (½in). Heat in the oven for 5 minutes. Add the potatoes and sprinkle lightly with salt. Roast for 40 minutes until crisp and cooked, occasionally turning and basting the potatoes.
Serves 2

Crispy Leeks

375g (12oz) leeks, cut into 4cm (1½in) lengths

1 bouquet garni

2 cloves

15g (½oz) butter

90ml (3fl oz) vegetable stock

3 tblspn dry white wine

salt

freshly ground black pepper

2-3 tblspn single cream

3-4 tblspn fresh wholemeal breadcrumbs

1 Place the leeks in a saucepan with the bouquet garni, cloves, butter, stock and wine. Add salt and pepper to taste. Bring to the boil, lower the heat and simmer for 10-12 minutes.

2 Using a slotted spoon, transfer the leeks to a buttered shallow flameproof dish, discarding the cloves and bouquet garni. Boil the cooking juices until reduced by half, then stir in the cream.

3 Pour the pan juices over the leeks, top them with the breadcrumbs and cook under a preheated moderately hot grill until the topping is crisp and golden.
Serves 2

Green Beans with Dijon Mustard

250g (8oz) French beans, topped and tailed

salt

15g (1/2oz) butter

2 tspn chopped parsley

1 spring onion, chopped

1-1½ tspn Dijon mustard

2 tspn water

1 Cook the beans in a saucepan with boiling water to cover until crisp-tender. Drain and sprinkle lightly with salt.

2 Melt the butter in the clean, dry saucepan and fry the parsley and spring onion gently for 1 minute. Stir in the mustard and measured water. Add the beans, turn to coat in the sauce, heat through and serve.

Serves 2

Puréed Carrots

500g (1lb) carrots, diced

5 tblspn vegetable stock

45g (1½oz) butter, softened

salt

freshly ground black pepper

2 tblspn single cream

1 Combine the carrots and stock in a saucepan. Bring to the boil, cover tightly, lower the heat and simmer until the carrots are very tender.

French Roast Chicken with Cream Gravy

2 Remove the lid and cook until most of the liquid has evaporated.

3 Transfer the mixture to a blender or food processor, add the butter and work to a purée.

4 Return to the clean pan, add salt and pepper to taste and reheat gently. Stir in the cream just before serving.

Serves 2

Kitchen Tip

Dust the puréed carrots with freshly grated nutmeg; the flavours are complementary.

Light Chocolate Cups with Chestnut Mousse

Either of these delicious desserts would make the perfect finale to a festive meal for two.

110g (3½oz) white chocolate, melted

Filling

75g (2½oz) chestnut purée

30g (1oz) butter, softened

1 tblspn Tia Maria

90g (3oz) cream cheese, softened

2 tblspn icing sugar

60g (2oz) dark chocolate, melted

1 Using paper patty cases double for extra support, brush 4 paper cases with the melted white chocolate. Chill until set, peel off the paper cases and reserve the chocolate cups in the refrigerator.

2 In a blender or food processor, process the chestnut purée with the butter, Tia Maria, cream cheese and icing sugar until smooth. With the motor running, pour in the melted chocolate. Spoon the mixture into a bowl and chill for 1 hour until firm.

3 Divide the mixture between the chocolate cups; chill until ready to serve.
Serves 2

Meringue Nests

3 egg whites

¼ tspn cream of tartar

220g (7oz) caster sugar

whipped cream and fresh fruit to serve

1 Preheat oven to 120°C (250°F/ Gas ½). Line two baking sheets with nonstick baking parchment. Using a glass as a guide, draw twelve 6cm (2½ in) circles.

Meringue Nests

2 Beat the egg whites in a grease-free bowl until frothy, then add the cream of tartar and beat until stiff peaks form.

3 Beat in 2 tablespoons of the caster sugar, then continue beating until the mixture is stiff and glossy. Fold in the remaining sugar, using a metal spoon.

4 Spoon the meringue into a piping bag fitted with a large plain or star tube. Pipe the meringue to fill in the circles on the paper, then pipe circles around the edges to form nests.

5 Bake for 1 hour, then turn off the oven. Carefully invert the meringue nests on the baking sheets and return them to the oven until cool. Fill 1 meringue per person with fruit and cream just before serving.

Serves 2

VEGETARIAN CHOICE

It is easy to integrate vegetarian guests when planning a Christmas feast. After a suitable starter, offer a variety of vegetables to appeal to all palates, and add a main attraction such as Mushroom and Hazelnut Roulade or Festive Filo Slice.

Leek and Stilton Soufflés

Illustrated on page 9

60g (2oz) butter

250g (8oz) leeks, finely chopped

2 tblspn flour

140ml (4½fl oz) milk

185g (6oz) Stilton cheese, grated

½ tspn dry mustard

salt

freshly ground black pepper

4 eggs, separated

1 Preheat oven to 190°C (375°F/ Gas 5). Melt the butter in a saucepan and sauté the leeks for 2-3 minutes until softened. Stir in the flour and cook for 1 minute, stirring constantly.

2 Gradually add the milk, stirring until the sauce boils and thickens.

3 Add the grated cheese and mustard, with salt and pepper to taste. Stir until the cheese has melted, then cool slightly. Stir in the egg yolks.

4 Whisk the egg whites in a grease-free bowl until stiff peaks form. Stir a little of the whisked egg into the cheese mixture to lighten it, then fold in the remainder, taking care not to over-mix.

5 Divide the mixture between four oiled 300ml (10fl oz) soufflé dishes. Bake for 25 minutes until risen, golden brown and just firm. Serve at once.
Serves 4

Mushroom and Hazelnut Roulade

90g (3oz) butter

60g (2oz) flour

500ml (16fl oz) milk, warmed

salt

freshly ground black pepper

2 tblspn single cream

4 eggs, separated

Filling

60g (2oz) hazelnuts

90g (3oz) butter

250g (8oz) mushrooms, sliced

30g (1oz) flour

250ml (8fl oz) milk

¼ tspn grated nutmeg

125ml (4fl oz) single cream

2 tblspn chopped parsley

1 Preheat oven to 160°C (325°F/ Gas 3). Line a 30 x 25cm (12 x 10in) Swiss Roll tin with greased nonstick baking parchment. Melt the butter in a saucepan, stir in the flour and cook for 1 minute. Gradually add the milk, stirring until the mixture boils and thickens. Off the heat, stir in salt and pepper to taste. Add the cream, then beat in the egg yolks, a little at a time.

2 Whisk the egg whites in a grease-free bowl until soft peaks form; fold into the egg yolk mixture. Spoon into the tin, tilting it to make sure the mixture reaches the corners. Bake for 25-35 minutes, until golden and firm to the touch.

3 Meanwhile make the filling. Cook the hazelnuts until a preheated grill until golden, then chop in a blender or food processor.

4 Melt the butter in a saucepan, add the mushrooms and cook over moderately high heat for 3 minutes. Stir in the flour and cook for 1 minute, then gradually add the milk, stirring until the sauce boils and thickens. Season to taste with salt, pepper and the nutmeg, then stir in the cream, parsley and ground hazelnuts.

5 Run a knife around the edge of the roulade and turn it out onto a sheet of nonstick baking parchment placed on top of a tea-towel.

6 Lift off the lining paper from the roulade, spread with the hot mushroom and hazelnut mixture and roll up, using the paper and tea-towel as a guide. Transfer to a platter and serve.
Serves 6-8

Kitchen Tip
The roulade may be made several hours in advance, covered with clingfilm and foil, then refrigerated until required. Bring to room temperature and remove the wrappings. Cover with fresh foil and reheat in a 150°C (300°F/Gas 2) oven for about 30 minutes.

Festive Filo Slice

375g (12oz) broccoli, cut into large pieces

500g (1lb) carrots, sliced

125g (4oz) red lentils

30g (1oz) butter

1 onion, roughly chopped

2 cloves garlic, crushed

125g (4oz) ground almonds

60g (2oz) mature Cheddar cheese, grated

4 eggs

1 red pepper, finely chopped

salt

freshly ground black pepper

½ tspn curry powder

30g (1oz) fresh white breadcrumbs

5 sheets of filo pastry, thawed if frozen

oil for brushing

grated Parmesan cheese for dusting

Sauce

1 red pepper, chopped

2 cloves garlic, crushed

½ green or red chilli, seeded and sliced

2 tblspn chopped fresh breadcrumbs

5 tblspn olive oil

Garnish

whole red chillies

parsley sprigs

1 Preheat oven to 180°C (350°F/ Gas 4). Line and grease a 1kg (2lb) loaf tin.

2 Cook the broccoli in a saucepan of boiling salted water until tender; drain well. Cook the carrots in a separate pan of boiling water for 10 minutes. Add the lentils to the carrots and cook for 10 minutes more or until the carrots are tender; drain.

3 Melt the butter in a saucepan and cook the onion and garlic over gentle heat for 3 minutes. Tip the mixture into a blender or food processor, add the broccoli and ground almonds and purée until smooth.

4 Transfer the purée to a bowl and beat in the cheese with 2 of the eggs. Stir in the red pepper, add salt and pepper to taste and spoon the mixture into the prepared tin.

5 Purée the carrot and lentil mixture with the remaining eggs, curry powder and breadcrumbs until smooth. Add salt and pepper to taste. Spoon into the tin and, using a teaspoon, swirl the mixtures together lightly.

6 Cover the tin with foil and bake for 1 hour. When cool, remove the loaf from the tin.

7 Reheat the oven to 180°C (350°F/Gas 4). Wrap the loaf like a parcel in a sheet of filo. Brush lightly with oil. Repeat the process three times more, brushing each filo wrapping lightly with oil.

8 Transfer the loaf to a baking sheet. Lay the remaining filo sheet over the top, easing the pastry into soft folds. Brush lightly with oil and bake for 30 minutes, covering the loaf lightly with foil as soon as the filo has turned golden.

9 Meanwhile make the sauce. Combine the red pepper, garlic, chilli and breadcrumbs in a blender or food processor. Blend to a paste. With the motor running, add the oil gradually, blending until smooth.

10 Transfer the loaf to a warmed platter. Dust with Parmesan. Serve in slices, with the sauce. Garnish each portion with a chilli and a sprig of parsley.

Serves 6-8

Festive Filo Slice

BOXING DAY

Enjoy your easiest ever Boxing Day with this selection of delicious dishes. The traditional glazed ham is the centrepiece of a spread that includes something for everyone – without a trace of turkey!

Honey-glazed Ham

These tender slices of perfectly cooked ham are popular with guests of all ages.

4.9kg (9lb) cooked leg of ham

155g (5oz) clear honey

250ml (8fl oz) freshly squeezed orange juice

1 tblspn Dijon mustard

2 tspn soy sauce

1 tblspn soft brown sugar

whole cloves

watercress to garnish

1 Preheat oven to 180°C (350°F/ Gas 4). Remove the skin from the ham: starting at the broad end, gently ease the skin away from the fat; it should come off in one complete piece.

2 Holding the ham firmly in one hand, score the fat in a diamond pattern, using a sharp knife. Avoid cutting the meat.

3 Place the ham in a large roasting tin. Combine the honey, orange juice, mustard, soy sauce and brown sugar in a bowl, mix well, then brush about a quarter of the mixture over the surface of the ham.

4 Stud each diamond in the fat with a whole clove. Bake for 1 hour, brushing the ham every 20 minutes with the remaining glaze and the cooking juices.

Honey-glazed Ham

5 If the ham is to be served hot, allow it to rest for 5 minutes, then transfer to a warmed serving platter and garnish with watercress.

6 If the ham is to be served cold, it may be glazed the day before and refrigerated, but should be brought to room temperature before carving. Serve with mustard, a selection of pickles and Apricot and Orange Relish (recipe follows).
Serves 20-24

Apricot and Orange Relish

185g (6oz) no-need-to-soak dried apricots

300ml (10fl oz) unsweetened orange juice

2 tblspn white wine vinegar

1 tblspn clear honey

1 tspn cornflour dissolved in 2 tspn water

salt

freshly ground black pepper

pinch of grated nutmeg or ground ginger

1 Bring the apricots, orange juice, vinegar and honey to the boil in a saucepan, then lower the heat and simmer for 5 minutes until soft and pulpy.

2 Purée the mixture in a blender or food processor, return to the clean pan and stir in the cornflour mixture. Reheat gently, stirring constantly until thickened. Add salt, pepper and nutmeg or ginger to taste. Serve hot or cold.
Makes about 375ml (12fl oz)

Marinated Mushrooms

500g (1lb) small button mushrooms

375ml (12fl oz) water

2 tblspn lemon juice

60ml (2fl oz) cider vinegar

1 tblspn dried mixed peppercorns

2 cloves garlic, crushed

1 tspn caster sugar

1 bay leaf

salt to taste

few sprigs fresh dill or tarragon

1 Trim the mushroom stalks and wipe the caps with damp paper towels. Put the caps in a saucepan with the measured water and lemon juice. Bring to the boil, cook for 1 minute, then drain well.

2 Place the mushrooms in a clean jar with a tight-fitting lid. Combine the remaining ingredients and pour over the mushrooms to cover them completely. Close the lid tightly. Store in the refrigerator for 1 week before serving.
Serves 6-8

Creamy Potato Layer

6 large potatoes, thinly sliced

salt

freshly ground black pepper

grated nutmeg

30g (1oz) butter, diced

155ml (5fl oz) single cream

1 Bring a large saucepan of salted water to the boil. Add the potatoes. When the water returns to the boil, cook for 1 minute, then drain the potatoes well.

2 Layer the potatoes in a large gratin dish, sprinkling each layer with salt, pepper and nutmeg, and dotting with butter. Pour the cream over the top. Bake for 45-60 minutes, or until golden.
Serves 6-8

Stilton and Watercress Tart

250g (8oz) plain flour

¼ tspn salt

125g (4oz) butter or margarine

about 3 tblspn cold water

salad leaves and radishes to serve

Filling

30g (1oz) butter

2 bunches watercress, leaves stripped from stalks

315g (10oz) Stilton cheese, rind removed, diced

3 eggs

155g (5oz) single cream

salt

freshly ground black pepper

1 Preheat oven to 200°C (400°F/ Gas 6). Sift the flour and salt into a large bowl. Rub in the butter or margarine until the mixture resembles breadcrumbs, then add enough water to mix to a firm dough.

2 Roll out the pastry on a lightly floured surface and use to line an oiled 20cm (8in) flan tin. Prick the base, chill for 15 minutes, then bake blind for 10-12 minutes. Lower the oven temperature to 180°C (350°F/Gas 4).

3 Meanwhile prepare the filling. Melt the butter in a large frying pan. Cook the watercress leaves for 10-12 minutes, stirring constantly until just wilted. Drain, pressing the watercress against the strainer to remove the excess liquid. Arrange in the flan shell and dot with the Stilton cubes.

4 Beat the eggs and cream in a bowl, add salt and pepper to taste and pour into the flan shell. Bake for 30-35 minutes until set. Serve warm or cold with salad leaves and chives.
Serves 4-6

Three Cheese Pizza

Pizzas are a popular choice, especially as far as the younger guests are concerned.

15g (½ oz) dried yeast

125ml (4fl oz) warm water

500g (1lb) plain flour

¼ tspn salt

2 tblspn olive oil

Topping

45g (1½oz) butter

2 large onions, sliced

3 tomatoes, skinned and chopped

2 tblspn chopped fresh basil

125g (4oz) Stilton cheese, crumbled

125g (4oz) mozzarella cheese, sliced

125g (4oz) Red Leicester or Cheddar cheese, grated

1 Dissolve the yeast in the measured water in a small bowl. Set aside until frothy. Meanwhile, sift the flour and salt into a mixing bowl.

2 Add the oil and yeast liquid to the flour mixture and mix to a smooth dough, adding a little extra water if necessary. Knead on a lightly floured surface until smooth and elastic, then divide the dough in half and roll into two 20cm (8in) circles. Place on oiled baking sheets, cover loosely with clingfilm and leave to rise in a warm place for 20 minutes.

3 Preheat oven to 200°C (400°F/ Gas 6). Melt the butter in a large frying pan, add the onions and cook gently for 10 minutes.

4 Divide the tomatoes and the onion mixture between the two pizza bases. Sprinkle each with basil. Arrange the cheeses on top and bake for 25-30 minutes.
Serves 6-8

Kitchen Tip
Make mini pizzas for young children, if preferred. Allow them to add their own toppings.

Celebration Salad

1 large head curly endive

1 bunch young spinach

2-3 sticks celery

1 Spanish onion, thinly sliced

2 grapefruit, peeled, pith removed, chopped

60g (2oz) flaked almonds, toasted

Dressing

1½ tspn honey

5 tblspn lemon juice

155ml (5fl oz) olive oil

salt and freshly ground black pepper

1 Wash the endive and spinach leaves carefully. Dry well, either in a salad spinner or between paper towels. If not using immediately, wrap in paper towels and store in a polythene bag in the refrigerator.

2 When ready to serve, place the endive and spinach leaves in a large salad bowl. Add the celery, onion and grapefruit and mix to combine.

3 Make the dressing. Mix the honey, lemon juice and olive oil in a screwtop jar. Close the lid tightly and shake to combine. Add salt and pepper to taste.

Stilton and Watercress Tart, Three Cheese Pizza

4 Add enough of the dressing to the salad to coat the leaves. Toss gently, sprinkle with the toasted almonds and serve at once.
Serves 6-8

Variation
Substitute oranges for the grapefruit and 2 crumbled grilled rindless bacon rashers for the almonds, if preferred.

Teatime Treats

No matter how much we indulge ourselves during the great festive splurge, we always seem to have enough room for the cakes and bakes that are such an important part of the Christmas tradition.

Royal-iced Christmas Cake

Decorate the cake with Santa Claus and Christmas trees, or add a more sophisticated topping with presents and pearls. A narrow ribbon completes the effect.

750g (1½lb) mixed dried fruit

125g (4oz) glacé cherries, chopped

125g (4oz) dried apricots, chopped

90g (3oz) stoned prunes, chopped

60g (2oz) Brazil nuts, chopped

grated rind and juice of 1 lemon

3 tblspn brandy

220g (7oz) butter, softened

220g (7oz) soft dark brown sugar

280g (9oz) plain flour

2 tspn mixed spice

60g (2oz) ground almonds

1½ tblspn black treacle

4 eggs, beaten

750g (1½lb) white marzipan

icing sugar for dusting

3 tblspn apricot jam, boiled and sieved

Royal Icing

2 egg whites

2 tspn glycerine

1 tspn lemon juice

500g (1lb) icing sugar, sifted

1 Line a 20cm (8in) round cake tin, following the instructions in Kitchen Tip, right. Preheat oven to 140°C (275°C/Gas 1).

2 Combine the mixed dried fruit, cherries, apricots, prunes, nuts, lemon rind, juice and brandy in a large bowl. Mix well.

3 In a separate, larger bowl, cream the butter with the sugar. Add the flour, spice, almonds, treacle and eggs. Beat with a wooden spoon for 1-2 minutes until smooth and glossy. Stir in the fruit mixture.

4 Spoon the mixture into the prepared cake tin, smooth the surface and bake for 3-3½ hours, or until a skewer inserted in the centre of the cake comes out clean.

5 Cool the cake in the tin, then invert onto a wire rack. Remove the lining paper, dust off any crumbs and transfer the cake to a 25cm (10in) cake board.

6 Roll out the marzipan on a surface lightly dusted with icing sugar to a 25cm (10in) round. Brush the cake with apricot jam, then cover with the marzipan, trimming any excess marzipan from the base of the cake. Set the cake aside for at least 1 week before adding the royal icing.

7 To make the royal icing, combine the egg whites, glycerine and lemon juice in a bowl. Gradually beat in the icing sugar until the icing peaks slightly. Spread the icing over the cake. Press a palette knife into the icing and pull away sharply to form peaks, leaving a plain band around the sides for the ribbon.

8 Tie the ribbon around the cake and decorate as wished.

Serves 24

Kitchen Tip

To line the cake tin, cut a circle of greaseproof paper to fit the base of the tin, then a strip long enough to go right around the sides of the tin and extending some 5cm (2in) above it. Make 4cm (1½in) slantwise cuts along one long edge of this strip. Grease the tin and fit the long strip around the sides, with the snipped margin lying flat against the bottom of the tin. Fit the greaseproof paper circle on top and grease the paper lining lightly but thoroughly.

Nonstick baking parchment may be used instead of greaseproof paper, if preferred.

Cranberry and Clementine Cake

185g (6oz) self-raising flour

185g (6oz) caster sugar

185g (6oz) butter, softened

3 eggs, lightly beaten

125g (4oz) cranberries

Frosting and Decoration

2 clementines

185g (6oz) butter, softened

375g (12oz) icing sugar, sifted

2 tblspn water

1 tblspn caster sugar

1 Line and grease two 20cm (8in) round sandwich tins. Preheat oven to 160°C (325°F/Gas 3).

2 Mix the flour, sugar, butter and eggs in a bowl. Beat with a wooden spoon for 1-2 minutes until smooth and glossy. Set aside 8 cranberries; chop the rest and stir them into the mixture.

3 Divide the mixture between the prepared tins and level the surfaces. Bake for 35-40 minutes or until the cakes spring back when lightly pressed with a finger. Cool on a wire rack.

4 To make the frosting, finely grate 1 clementine; place the rind in a bowl. Add the butter and mix well. Thinly pare the rind from the remaining clementine; set it aside. Squeeze both clementines to yield 2 tablespoons juice; add this to the bowl with the icing sugar and beat until fluffy.

5 Place 4 tablespoons of the frosting in a piping bag fitted with a small star nozzle.

Royal-iced Christmas Cake, Cranberry and Clementine Cake

6 Sandwich the cake layers together, using a third of the frosting, and spread the remainder over the top and sides. Pipe a frosting lattice and border on top of the cake.

7 Make the decoration. Heat the measured water and sugar in a small saucepan, then add the finely pared clementine rind. Simmer for 30 seconds; remove the rind with a slotted spoon and set aside. Add the reserved cranberries and cook gently for 30 seconds. Leave until cold, then use the cranberries and clementine rind to decorate the top of the cake.

Serves 8-12

Christmas Stollen

The quantities below make two Stollen; one to keep and one to give away.

375g (12oz) mixed dried fruit

90g (3oz) blanched almonds, chopped

2 tblspn dark rum

30g (1oz) fresh yeast

60ml (2fl oz) lukewarm water

125g (4oz) caster sugar

625g (1¼lb) plain flour

250ml (8fl oz) lukewarm milk

2 eggs, beaten

250g (8oz) butter, diced and softened, plus about 2 tblspn melted butter

½ tspn salt

beaten egg for glaze

sifted icing sugar to decorate

1 Combine the dried fruit, almonds and rum in a bowl. Set aside. Crumble the yeast into a jug or small bowl, Stir in the lukewarm water and 1 teaspoon of the sugar. Stir until the yeast dissolves, then set aside for 5 minutes until frothy.

2 Sift 250g (8oz) of the flour into a large mixing bowl. Stir in the yeast mixture and lukewarm milk. Cover with clingfilm and set aside in a warm place for about 1 hour, or until doubled in bulk. Preheat oven to 190°C (375°F/Gas 5).

3 Knock down the risen mixture firmly with your fist; work in the beaten eggs, remaining caster sugar and diced softened butter.

4 Sift the remaining flour with the salt. Work about two thirds of this mixture into the dough, using your hands. Then turn the dough out on a lightly floured surface and work in the remaining flour to form a smooth dough without any stickiness. Work in the fruit and nut mixture.

5 Divide the dough in half. On a lightly floured surface, pat or roll each portion to a thickness of 2cm (¾in) and shape each into an oval, about 30 x 20cm (12 x 8in).

6 Brush each oval with a little of the melted butter and fold the dough over lengthwise, almost in half. Lightly press the edges together to seal. Brush the tops with beaten egg. Bake for 35-40 minutes or until well risen and golden. Remove from the oven, place on wire racks and brush the tops again with the remaining melted butter. When cool, dust the Stollen generously with sifted icing sugar. Serve thickly sliced.

Makes 2

Buche Noel

60g (2oz) plain flour

½ tspn baking powder

¼ tspn salt

60g (2oz) dark chocolate, chopped

4 eggs

185g (6oz) caster sugar

1 tspn vanilla essence

2 tblspn warm water

¼ tspn bicarbonate of soda

icing sugar

Buttercream

185g (6oz) butter, softened

500g (1lb) icing sugar

4 tblspn cocoa

2-3 tblspn milk

1 Preheat oven to 200°C (400°F/Gas 6). Line and grease a 30 x 25cm (12 x 10in) Swiss Roll tin with greaseproof paper. Sift the flour, baking powder and salt onto a sheet of greaseproof paper; set the bowl aside.

2 Place the chocolate in a heatproof bowl; set over simmering water until melted. Remove from the heat, stir and set the bowl aside.

3 Beat the eggs with the caster sugar in a large mixing bowl until thick and light. This will take about 5 minutes with a hand-held electric mixer – when ready, the beaters should leave a trail in the mixture when lifted.

4 Add the sifted flour and vanilla essence all at once; fold in gently and quickly with a metal spoon. Add the warm water and bicarbonate of soda to the melted chocolate and stir until thick and smooth. Pour into the egg mixture and fold in until just combined. Do not beat the mixture.

5 Pour the mixture into the prepared tin, tilting it to make sure the mixture reaches the corners. Bake for 25-30 minutes, until golden and firm to the touch.

6 Place a sheet of greaseproof paper on top of a clean tea-towel. Dust the paper lightly with icing sugar. Run a knife around the edge of the sponge and turn it out onto the paper. Lift off the lining paper from the sponge and, using the tea-towel as a guide, roll up the sponge from one short side, with the greaseproof paper inside. Place on a wire rack until cold.

7 Make the buttercream by beating the butter until light, then adding the sifted icing sugar and cocoa. Beat until smooth and creamy, adding enough of the milk to give a spreading consistency. Carefully unroll the sponge, remove the paper and spread with half the buttercream. Roll the sponge up again.

8 Cut two 1cm (½in) slices on the slant from the roll and arrange on top to resemble a log. Frost the entire cake with the remaining buttercream, using a fork to mark whorls and lines resembling bark. Chill until ready to serve. Decorate as liked.

Serves 10-12

Kitchen Tip

Bake the Buche Noel mixture as soon as possible after combining the ingredients; bicarbonate of soda is activated as soon as it is combined with a liquid.

Christmas Stollen

Cherry Madeira Cake

185g (6oz) butter, softened

185g (6oz) caster sugar

3 eggs, beaten

185g (6oz) self-raising flour

60g (2oz) ground almonds

155g (5oz) glacé cherries, finely chopped

1 Preheat oven to 160°C (325°F/ Gas 3). Line and grease an 18cm (7in) round cake tin.

2 Cream the butter with the sugar in a bowl until light and fluffy. Gradually add the eggs, beating after each addition. Sift in the flour. Add the ground almonds and chopped glacé cherries; fold carefully into the mixture.

3 Spoon the mixture into the prepared tin and smooth the surface. Bake for 1-1¼ hours. Cool in the tin for 5 minutes, then turn out onto a wire rack, remove the paper, invert the cake and leave until cold.

Serves 12

Kitchen Tip

An apricot glaze, made by boiling and sieving 2 tablespoons apricot jam, may be brushed over the cooled cake. Decorate with halved glacé cherries and glacé pineapple pieces, then brush with the apricot glaze again.

Midweek Celebration

When spirits – and funds – begin to flag between Christmas and New Year, lift the mood with a party that's as easy on the purse as it is on the palate.

Turkey Creole

Adjust the amount of chilli powder to suit your personal taste. If preferred, add a few drops of Tabasco sauce, stirring it into the tomato juice.

30g (1oz) butter

2 cloves garlic, crushed

1 onion, finely chopped

2 tblspn flour

1-2 tspn chilli powder

300ml (10fl oz) tomato juice

300ml (10fl oz) chicken stock

750g (1½lb) cooked turkey, chopped

250g (8oz) mushrooms, sliced

salt

freshly ground black pepper

Garnish

cayenne pepper

bay leaves

1 Melt the butter in a saucepan and sauté the garlic and onion over gentle heat until softened. Stir in the flour and chilli powder. Cook for 1 minute, stirring.

2 Gradually add the tomato juice and chicken stock, stirring until the sauce boils and thickens.

3 Stir in the turkey and mushrooms, with salt and pepper to taste. Bring to the boil, cook over high heat for 5 minutes, then lower the heat and simmer for 2 minutes more.

4 Serve on a bed of boiled rice or noodles, dusting the turkey mixture with cayenne and adding a bay leaf garnish.
Serves 8

Turkey and Chutney Loaf

375g (12oz) cooked turkey, finely chopped

90g (3oz) fresh white breadcrumbs

2 eggs

1 small onion, chopped

2 tblspn chutney

90ml (3fl oz) milk

2-3 tspn paprika

4 tblspn finely chopped parsley

Garnish

cherry tomatoes

chopped salad leaves

1 Preheat oven to 180°C (350°F/ Gas 4). Mix all the ingredients except the garnish in a large bowl.

2 Press the mixture into a greased 500g (1lb) loaf tin and bake for 35-40 minutes. Serve hot or cold, with the tomatoes and salad leaves as a garnish.
Serves 6

Ham and Potato Cakes

375g (12oz) ham, finely chopped

375g (12oz) potatoes, cooked and mashed

2 tblspn snipped chives

freshly ground black pepper

125g (4oz) flour

oil for shallow frying

8 slices fresh or drained canned pineapple

salad garnish (optional)

Clockwise from top right: *Turkey Creole, Turkey and Chutney Loaf, Ham and Potato Cakes, Ham and Turkey Niçoise and Ham and Mushroom Rolls*

1 Combine the ham, potato, chives and pepper in a bowl and mix well.

2 Shape the mixture into eight cakes; coat lightly in flour.

3 Heat the oil in a frying pan and fry the cakes on both sides until golden brown, allowing about 3 minutes per side.

4 Drain the ham and potato cakes on paper towels. Serve hot, with the pineapple rings. Add a salad garnish if liked.
Serves 8

Ham and Turkey Niçoise

750g (1½lb) small new potatoes

salt

125g (4oz) French beans, topped and tailed

125g (4oz) cooked turkey, cut into strips

250g (8oz) ham, cut into strips

8 black olives

125g (4oz) cherry tomatoes, halved

4 spring onions, sliced diagonally

2 hard-boiled eggs, quartered

Dressing

2 tblspn red wine vinegar

½ clove garlic, crushed

1 tblspn wholegrain mustard

pinch sugar

75ml (2½fl oz) olive oil

1 Cook the potatoes in a saucepan of boiling salted water for 10-12 minutes until just cooked. Drain and allow to cool.

2 Blanch the beans in a small saucepan of salted boiling water for 2 minutes, drain and refresh under cold running water. Pat potatoes and beans dry on paper towels, then transfer to a large serving bowl.

3 Add the turkey, ham, olives, cherry tomatoes, spring onions and eggs to the bowl.

4 Make the dressing. Mix the vinegar, garlic, mustard and sugar in a bowl. Whisk in the olive oil gradually. Pour over the salad and toss gently to mix. Serve the salad at once.
Serves 4-6

Variation
Use garlic and red pepper mustard for the dressing, if available. It gives a rich colour and tangy flavour. Omit the crushed garlic.

Ham and Mushroom Rolls

185g (6oz) cream cheese

185ml (6fl oz) soured cream

1 egg, lightly beaten

1 small onion, finely chopped

125g (4oz) cooked spinach, well drained and chopped

pinch grated nutmeg

pinch dry mustard

salt and freshly ground black pepper

8 large slices of cooked ham, trimmed

Mushroom Sauce

250ml (8fl oz) cream of mushroom soup

60ml (2fl oz) soured cream

1 Preheat oven to 180°C (350°F/ Gas 4). Combine the cheese, soured cream, egg, onion and spinach in a bowl. Add the nutmeg and mustard, with salt and pepper to taste; mix well.

2 Place about 2 tablespoons of filling on each slice of ham and roll up. Arrange the rolls, seam-side down, in a shallow baking dish.

3 Combine the mushroom soup and soured cream in a jug, add salt and pepper to taste and pour over the ham rolls.

4 Bake for 25 minutes. Serve, garnished with celery, if liked.
Serves 4

Ring out the old year and ring in the new with a selection of simple starters, followed by roast beef with port and nut stuffing. Also on the menu are several sinful desserts – a final fling before the resolutions take effect!

Chicken Liver Mousse

Individual chicken liver mousses with Melba toast make an easy-to-serve starter. If preferred, the mousse may be made in two larger dishes for the buffet table.

750g (1½lb) chicken livers, trimmed

salt

freshly ground black pepper

2 tblspn Marsala or brandy

2 tblspn olive oil

500g (1lb) butter, softened

250ml (8fl oz) double cream

250g (8oz) clarified butter, see Kitchen Tip, page 21

16 sage leaves

1 Rinse the trimmed chicken livers under cold water. Drain and pat dry with paper towels.

2 Place the livers in a shallow dish, sprinkle with salt and pepper and pour the Marsala or brandy and olive oil over the top. Cover closely and marinate for 1-2 hours in the refrigerator, if time permits.

3 Place a nonstick frying pan over a low heat. Add the chicken livers with the marinade. Cook gently for 10-12 minutes or until the livers are firm but still pink in the middle when pierced with a sharp knife; the livers should not brown. Cool slightly.

4 Transfer the livers, with the pan juices, to a blender or food processor. Process until smooth, gradually adding the butter through the feeder tube.

5 Add the cream, with salt and pepper to taste. Process for 3 seconds more.

6 Divide the mousse between eight individual ramekins, smooth the surface and cover each with a thin layer of melted clarified butter. As the butter begins to firm, press a couple of sage leaves gently into each mousse. Cool, then chill until set. Serve with salad leaves and Melba toast (recipe follows).
Serves 8

Melba Toast

Melba toast looks impressive, but is very easy to make. Simply toast thinly sliced bread on both sides, then carefully cut off the crusts. Holding a sharp, long-bladed knife parallel to a slice of toast, slice the toast in half to make two very thin slices, each with one untoasted side. This is easier than it sounds – because the bread is toasted on both sides, the knife will naturally slide through the soft crumb of the middle.

Having halved all the toasted bread slices, place them, untoasted sides up, under a moderately hot grill. Watch them carefully and remove from the heat as soon as they become golden and curl at the edges. Take care as they burn very readily.

Serve Melba toast in a large bowl; a wooden salad bowl or pottery dish is ideal. Offer softened butter for those who wish to gild the lily.

Mushroom Filo Tartlets

4-6 sheets of filo pastry, thawed if frozen

155g (5oz) butter, melted

1 clove garlic, crushed

2 shallots, finely chopped

375g (12oz) mixed mushrooms, chopped

4 tblspn white wine

salt

freshly ground black pepper

herb sprigs to garnish

1 Preheat oven to 200°C (400°F/ Gas 6). Cut the filo pastry into 18 x 10cm (4in) squares.

2 Keeping the rest of the filo covered, lay a square in each of six individual 7.5cm (3in) flan tins or Yorkshire pudding tins. Brush with melted butter. Cover each square with a second filo square, moving the tins a one-third turn around. Repeat the process twice to make six filo cases, each three layers thick. Bake for 8-10 minutes until golden. Keep warm.

3 Meanwhile, heat the remaining butter in a frying pan. Sauté the garlic and shallots gently for 5 minutes until just golden. Add the mushrooms and wine, with salt and pepper to taste. Cook over high heat until most of the liquid has been absorbed.

4 Spoon the filling into the hot filo cases, garnish with the herb sprigs and serve at once.
Serves 6

Melon and Parma Ham

1 small Charentais melon

1 small Galia or Ogen melon

12 very thin slices of Parma ham

Dressing

60g (2oz) dolcelatte cheese

2 tblspn lemon juice

1-2 tspn olive oil

1-2 tblspn single cream

freshly ground black pepper

1 Cut both melons in half, scoop out the seeds, then cut into thin wedges. Neatly slice the skin off each wedge.

2 Arrange the melon wedges on individual serving plates with the Parma ham. Cover and chill.

3 Make the dressing. Mash the dolcelatte and lemon juice to a paste, then stir in the olive oil, cream and pepper to taste.

4 Just before serving, whisk the dressing, spoon it over the melon and garnish as desired.

Serves 4-6

Chicken Liver Mousse, Mushroom Filo Tartlets, Melon and Parma Ham

Variation
Fresh figs, cut almost but not quite through into quarters, may be used instead of the melon wedges. Open the figs out so that they look like flowers.

Roast Beef with Port and Nut Stuffing

1.5kg (3lb) fillet of beef, in one piece, trimmed

1 large carrot, roughly chopped

3 sticks celery, roughly chopped

1 large onion, roughly chopped

30g (1oz) butter, diced

250ml (8fl oz) beef stock

125ml (4fl oz) port

Stuffing

30g (1oz) walnuts, chopped

30g (1oz) butter, melted

2 tblspn chopped fresh parsley

2 tblspn clear honey

1 tblspn grated orange rind

60ml (2fl oz) port

1 egg, beaten

salt

freshly ground black pepper

about 125g (4oz) fresh white breadcrumbs

1 Preheat oven to 200°C (400°F/ Gas 6). Trim the beef, removing all fat and sinews. Make a lengthwise incision to form a pocket for stuffing, cutting only three quarters of the way through.

2 Combine all the stuffing ingredients in a bowl, adding enough of the breadcrumbs to make a moist, but not wet, stuffing.

3 Fill the pocket with the stuffing. Tie the beef at 5cm (2in) intervals with fine string to keep the stuffing in place.

4 Scatter the carrot, celery and onion on the bottom of a roasting tin. Dot the vegetables with butter. Place the beef on top. Roast for 50-60 minutes for rare beef, turning halfway through cooking. Transfer the beef to a warmed serving plate, cover loosely with foil and allow to rest for 15 minutes before carving.

5 Strain the pan juices through a sieve into a saucepan, pressing down on the vegetables to extract as much liquid as possible. Add the beef stock and port to the pan and bring to the boil. Cook over high heat until the liquid is reduced to the consistency of thin gravy. Add salt and pepper to taste.

6 Remove the strings from the beef. Spoon a little gravy over the beef and garnish with watercress. Carve the beef into neat, thick slices, Serve at once, offering the remaining gravy in a warmed gravyboat.

Serves 8-10

Herby Roast Potatoes

1kg (2lb) potatoes, cut into small even-sized chunks

flour for coating

2 eggs, beaten

2 cloves garlic, crushed

grated rind of 1 large lemon

salt

freshly ground black pepper

125-155g (4-5oz) sage and onion stuffing mix or dried breadcrumbs

lard or oil for roasting

1 Preheat oven to 200°C (400°F/ Gas 6). Bring a saucepan of salted water to the boil, add the potatoes and cook for 5 minutes. Drain and pat dry with paper towels. Cool slightly.

2 Spread out the flour for coating in a shallow bowl. Mix the eggs, garlic and lemon rind in a second shallow bowl. Add salt and pepper. Finally spread out the dry stuffing mix or breadcrumbs on a sheet of greaseproof paper.

3 Coat the potatoes with flour, dip them in the egg mixture, then coat in the stuffing mix, pressing it on well.

4 Heat the lard or oil in a roasting tin for 10 minutes, then add the potatoes and baste well. Roast for about 45 minutes, turning once. Drain on paper towels, transfer to a heated dish and serve.

Serves 6

Celery with Bay and Bacon

1 head celery

salt

30g (1oz) butter

1 small onion, chopped

2 rindless back bacon rashers, chopped

2 bay leaves

freshly ground black pepper

1 Trim the celery. Cut the sticks into 7.5cm (3in) lengths, then into broad strips. Cook in a saucepan of boiling water for 10 minutes, then drain, reserving 3 tablespoons of the cooking liquid.

2 Heat the butter in a large frying pan and cook the onion for about 5 minutes until softened. Add the bacon and cook for 5 minutes more, until slightly crisp. Add the celery and bay leaves, with salt and pepper to taste, and pour in the reserved cooking liquid. Cover the pan; simmer for 20 minutes, until the celery is tender. Serve hot.

Serves 6

Red Cabbage

2 tblspn sunflower oil

1 head red cabbage, shredded

2 Bramley apples, peeled and chopped

500ml (16fl oz) hot water

125ml (4fl oz) cider vinegar

60g (2oz) soft brown sugar

6 juniper berries, bruised

½ tspn salt

1 Heat the oil in a large saucepan, add the cabbage and apples and cook over moderate heat for 3 minutes.

2 Stir in all the remaining ingredients. Bring to the boil, then simmer over the lowest possible heat for about 1 hour.

Serves 6

Puffed Parsnip Bake

500g (1lb) parsnips

salt

freshly ground black pepper

60g (2oz) butter

3 tblspn single cream

¼ tspn grated nutmeg

1 egg, beaten

2 tblspn wholemeal breadcrumbs

1 Preheat oven to 180°C (350°F/ Gas 4). Cut the parsnips in half lengthwise, removing any woody core, then chop into chunks. Bring a saucepan of salted water to the boil, add the parsnips and cook for 15-20 minutes until tender. Drain well in a colander.

2 Mash the parsnips with half the butter. Add the cream, nutmeg and egg, with salt and pepper to taste. Mix well. Turn the mixture into a buttered ovenproof dish.

Roast Beef with Port and Nut Stuffing

3 Melt the remaining butter and pour it over the dish. Sprinkle with breadcrumbs and bake for 20-25 minutes until puffed up and golden brown.
Serves 4-6

Chestnut Bavarois

7g (¼oz) powdered gelatine

250ml (8fl oz) milk

250g (8oz) canned unsweetened chestnut purée

3 egg yolks

90g (3oz) caster sugar

470ml (15fl oz) whipping cream

Decoration

whipped cream

4 marrons glacés

1 Chill a 900ml (1½pt) charlotte tin. Sprinkle the gelatine onto 2 tablespoons cold water in a heatproof bowl. When spongy, melt over hot water.

2 Place the milk in a saucepan with half the chestnut purée. Bring to the boil. Meanwhile, whisk the egg yolks in a bowl with 60g (2oz) of the sugar until thick and light. Stir in a little of the hot milk mixture, then add this to the remaining milk mixture. Cook, stirring constantly over low heat until the custard thickens enough to coat the back of the spoon. Do not allow the custard to boil.

3 Add the gelatine to the hot custard and mix well. Cool, then chill until on the point of setting.

4 Whip the cream in a bowl until soft peaks form. Set aside. Place the remaining chestnut purée in a small bowl and break it up with a fork. Add the remaining sugar and beat until smooth. Fold in 2 tablespoons of the chilled custard and 1 tablespoon of the cream; set aside.

5 Fold the remaining cream into the chilled custard and pour half of this into the chilled charlotte tin. Chill until set.

Iced Cointreau Soufflé (page 46), Chestnut Bavarois and Speedy Lemon Mousse

6 Spoon the chestnut purée onto the set bavarois and spread evenly with the back of the spoon. Top with the remaining bavarois mixture. Chill until completely set, then unmould onto a chilled plate. Decorate with whipped cream and marrons glacés and serve.
Serves 6-8

Speedy Lemon Mousse

375ml (12fl oz) condensed milk

300ml (10fl oz) whipping cream

grated rind and juice of 4 large lemons

Decoration

lemon slices

mint sprigs

1 Combine the condensed milk and cream in a large bowl. Whisk with a hand-held mixer until the mixture thickens slightly to leave a ribbon trail when the beaters are lifted.

2 Continue to whisk the mixture and slowly add the lemon rind and juice; the mixture will suddenly thicken.

3 Spoon into individual serving glasses and chill overnight. Decorate with lemon slices and mint sprigs just before serving.
Serves 6-8

Variations

This simple dessert may be made with a variety of citrus fruits. Substitute 3 oranges or 6 limes for the lemons, if preferred, and alter the decorations accordingly.

The mousse may also be served in lemon, orange or lime shells. Take a thin slice of the base of the chosen fruit so that each stands level, remove a larger slice from the top as a lid, and hollow out the centres. Fill with mousse, then replace the lids.

Iced Cointreau Soufflé

Illustrated on page 44

3 eggs, plus 2 egg yolks

155g (5oz) caster sugar

grated rind and juice of 1 orange

300ml (10fl oz) whipping cream

75ml (2½fl oz) Cointreau

Decoration

orange segments

orange rind shreds

1 Cut a piece of nonstick baking parchment at least 25cm (10in) deep and long enough to wrap around a 600ml (1pt) soufflé dish. Fold the paper in half lengthwise to give a 12cm (5in) band. Wrap this around the dish and secure with string. The collar should stand about 5cm (2in) above the dish.

Mulled Wine

2 Place the whole eggs, egg yolks, sugar, orange rind and juice in a large heatproof bowl. Stand over hot water and whisk constantly with a hand-held electric mixer until the mixture forms a thick ribbon when the beaters are lifted. Remove the bowl from the pan and leave to cool completely.

3 Whip the cream in a separate bowl until it is the same consistency as the whisked mixture. Fold a tablespoon of the cream into the mixture to lighten it, then fold in the remaining cream and Cointreau. Pour into the prepared dish and freeze overnight.

4 To serve, carefully remove the paper collar, smooth the edge and decorate with orange segments and shreds of orange rind. Offer a jug of cream.
Serves 10

Mulled Wine

250ml (8fl oz) water

1 cinnamon stick

6 cloves

6 allspice berries

1 bottle red wine

185ml (6fl oz) port

1 tblspn caster sugar

thinly pared rind of ½ lemon

lemon slices to serve

1 Simmer the water and spices in a saucepan for 20 minutes.

2 Pour the red wine into a second saucepan. Strain in the spiced water, reserving the spices. Add the port and sugar. Heat, stirring, until just below boiling point. Serve in a heatproof bowl, decorated with lemon rind, lemon slices and the reserved spices.
Serves 6-8

USEFUL INFORMATION

Length

Centimetres	Inches	Centimetres	Inches
0.5 (5mm)	¼	18	7
1	½	20	8
2	¾	23	9
2.5	1	25	10
4	1½	30	12
5	2	35	14
6	2½	40	16
7.5	3	45	18
10	4	50	20
15	6	NB: 1cm=10mm	

Metric/Imperial Conversion Chart

Mass (Weight)

(Approximate conversions for cookery purposes)

Metric	Imperial	Metric	Imperial
15g	½oz	315g	10oz
30g	1oz	350g	11oz
60g	2oz	375g	12oz (¾lb)
90g	3oz	410g	13oz
125g	4oz (¼lb)	440g	14oz
155g	5oz	470g	15oz
185g	6oz	500g (0.5kg)	16oz (1lb)
220g	7oz	750g	24oz (1½lb)
250g	8oz	1000g (1kg)	32oz (2lb)
280g	9oz	1500g (1.5kg)	48oz (3lb)

Metric Spoon Sizes

¼ teaspoon	= 1.25ml
½ teaspoon	= 2.5ml
1 teaspoon	= 5ml
1 tablespoon	= 15ml

Liquids

Metric	Imperial
30ml	1fl oz
60ml	2fl oz
90ml	3fl oz
125ml	4fl oz
155ml	5fl oz (¼ pt)
185ml	6fl oz
250ml	8fl oz
500ml	16fl oz
600ml	20fl oz (1pt)
750ml	1¼ pt
1 litre	1¾ pt
1.2 litres	2pt
1.5 litres	2½ pt
1.8 litres	3pt
2 litres	3½ pt
2.5 litres	4pt

Index

Almond Brussels Sprouts 14
Apple and Hazelnut Stuffing 13
Apples and Nightlights 7
Apricot and Orange Relish 31
Apricot Sherry Trifle 16
Bacon-wrapped Sausages 12
Beans with Tomato 16
Bishop's Bread 5
Bread Sauce 12
Buche Noel 36
Carrots and Celery 16
Celebration Salad 33
Celery with Bay and Bacon 42
Cherry Chutney 13
Cherry Madeira Cake 37
Chestnut Bavarois 45
Chicken Liver Mousse 40
Chocolate Truffles 21
Christmas Stollen 36
Christmas Tree Biscuits 4
Citrus Broccoli and Cauliflower 14
Clear Brandy Sauce 18
Cranberry and Clementine Cake 35
Creamy Potato Layer 32
Crispy Bacon and Avocado Salad 10
Crispy Leeks 24

Festive Filo Slice 28
Filo Crackers 20
French Roast Chicken with Cream Gravy 24
Fruit and Nut Caramels 4
Glazed Christmas Cake 3
Golden Advent Ring 6
Green Beans with Dijon Mustard 25
Ham and Asparagus Gratins 8
Ham and Mushroom Rolls 39
Ham and Potato Cakes 38
Ham and Turkey Niçoise 39
Herby Roast Potatoes 42
Holly and Nut Table Decoration 22
Honey Apple Sauce 13
Honey-glazed Ham 31
Iced Christmas Pudding 16
Iced Cointreau Soufflé 46
Indoor Wreaths 7
Kissing Ring 7
Leek and Stilton Soufflés 27
Light Chocolate Cups with Chestnut Mousse 26
Marinated Mushrooms 32
Melba Toast 40
Melon and Parma Ham 41
Meringue Nests 26
Mince Pies 20
Mulled Wine 46
Mushroom and Hazelnut Roulade 27

Mushroom Filo Tartlets 40
Napkin Garlands 23
Orange and Brandy Butter 18
Pan Gravy 12
Peppermint Creams 4
Perfect Roast Turkey 10
Pomanders 6
Puffed Parsnip Bake 43
Puréed Carrots 25
Quick Cumberland Sauce 12
Railroad Potatoes 24
Red Cabbage 42
Roast Beef with Port and Nut Stuffing 42
Rosemary Potatoes 14
Royal-iced Christmas Cake 34
Shortbread Jewels 4
Smoked Salmon Parcels 23
Speedy Lemon Mousse 45
Spicy Cranberry Sauce 13
Stilton and Watercress Tart 32
Striped Salmon Terrine 8
Studded Oranges 6
Three Cheese Pizza 32
Traditional Christmas Pudding 18
Turkey and Chutney Loaf 38
Turkey Creole 38

Published by Merehurst Limited
Ferry House
51-57 Lacy Road
Putney
London SW15 1PR

Cookery Editor: Jenni Fleetwood
Cover Design: Sue Rawkins
Cover Photography: Clive Streeter
Special Photography: James Duncan
Cover Home Economist: Kathy Man
Cover Stylist: Hilary Guy

Colour separation by Fotographics Limited UK - Hong Kong
Printed in Italy by G Canale & C SpA

ISBN 1 874567 82 4

Distribution and Sales Enquiries:
J.B. Fairfax Press Limited,
9 Trinity Centre, Park Farm Estate, Wellingborough, Northants, NN8 6ZB.
Ph (0933) 402330 Fax (0933) 402234